Sanders

Sanders

ENGLAND
the land

Erinn Banting

A Bobbie Kalman Book

The Lands, Peoples, and Cultures Series

Crabtree Publishing Company

www.crabtreebooks.com

The Lands, Peoples, and Cultures Series

Created by Bobbie Kalman

Coordinating editor
Ellen Rodger

Project editor
Sean Charlebois

Production coordinator
Rosie Gowsell

Project development, design, editing, and photo research
First Folio Resource Group, Inc.: Erinn Banting, Quinn Banting, Molly Bennett, Tom Dart, Greg Duhaney, Jaimie Nathan, Debbie Smith, Meighan Sutherland, Anikó Szocs

Editing
Carolyn Black

Prepress and printing
Worzalla Publishing Company

Consultants
Jane Higginbottom, Alex Lloyd, Chris Stephenson

Photographs
Art Archive/Jarrold Publishing: p. 15 (top); Bill Bachmann/ Photo Researchers: p. 12 (bottom); Tom Bean: cover; Annie Griffiths Belt/Corbis/magmaphoto.com: p. 4 (top), p. 27 (bottom); Birmingham Picture Library: p. 16 (left); Jonathan Blair/Corbis/magmaphoto.com: p. 14 (left); Peter Carmichael/ Aspect Picture Library Ltd: p. 23 (bottom); Anthony Cooper/ Ecoscene/Corbis/magmaphoto.com: p. 22 (top); Ashley Cooper/Picimpact/Corbis/magmaphoto.com: p. 6, p. 31 (top left); Tony Craddock/Photo Researchers: p. 5 (bottom); Derek Croucher/Corbis/magmaphoto.com: p. 5 (top); Grace Davies: p. 9 (right); Ric Ergenbright: p. 8 (left), p. 19 (bottom); Colin Garratt/Milepost 92 1/2/Corbis/magmaphoto.com: p. 17 (left), p. 26 (left), p. 29 (top); Anne Gordon: p. 13 (bottom); James A. Gordon/Anne Gordon Images: p. 28 (top); Brian Harding/ Eye Ubiquitous/Corbis/magmaphoto.com: p. 19 (top); Jim Hargan: title page, p. 20 (left); Jason Hawkes/Corbis/ magmaphoto.com: p. 26 (right); Robert Holmes/Corbis/ magmaphoto.com: p. 18 (left); Angelo Hornak/Corbis/ magmaphoto.com: p. 3, p. 11 (bottom); Hulton Archive/Getty Images.: p. 25 (bottom); Hulton-Deutsch Collection/Corbis/ magmaphoto.com: p. 25 (top); Jacqui Hurst/Corbis/ magmaphoto.com: p. 23 (top); Richard Klune/Corbis/ magmaphoto.com: p. 11 (top), p. 16 (right); Bob Krist/Corbis/ magmaphoto.com: p. 10; Susan McCartney/Photo Researchers: p. 12 (top); Will and Deni McIntyre/Photo Researchers: p. 13 (top), p. 14 (right); Allan A. Philiba: p. 20 (right); Benjamin Rondel/Corbis/ magmaphoto.com: p. 18 (right); Royalty-Free/Corbis/ magmaphoto.com: p. 15 (bottom), p. 31 (right and bottom left); Paul Seheult/Eye Ubiquitous/Corbis/ magmaphoto.com: p. 22 (bottom); Lee Snider/Corbis/ magmaphoto.com: p. 21 (bottom); Roger Tidman/Corbis/ magmaphoto.com: p. 30; Geoff Tompkinson/Aspect Picture Library Ltd: p. 27 (top); Patrick Ward/Corbis/magmaphoto.com: p. 7, p. 28 (bottom); Nik Wheeler/Corbis/magmaphoto.com: p. 4 (bottom); Terry Whittaker/Photo Researchers, Inc.: p. 8 (right); Jim Winkley/ Ecoscene/Corbis/magmaphoto.com: p. 29 (bottom); Adam Woolfitt/Corbis/magmaphoto.com: p. 17 (right), p. 21 (top); Michael S. Yamashita/Corbis/ magmaphoto.com: p. 9 (left)

Map
Jim Chernishenko

Illustrations
Dianne Eastman: icon
MikeCarterstudio.com: p. 24
David Wysotski, Allure Illustrations: back cover

Cover: Old stone buildings line a steep street in Shaftbury, a town in southern England.

Title page: Many English towns, such as Bridport, in the south, were built along the coast so they could be accessed by boat.

Icon: The Tower of London, which appears at the head of each section, has been used for hundreds of years as a fortress, a prison, and a royal residence.

Back cover: Red foxes live in wooded areas across England. These animals live alone unless they are raising their young.

Published by
Crabtree Publishing Company

PMB 16A,	612 Welland Avenue	73 Lime Walk
350 Fifth Avenue	St. Catharines	Headington
Suite 3308	Ontario, Canada	Oxford OX3 7AD
New York	L2M 5V6	United Kingdom
N.Y. 10118		

Cataloging-in-Publication data

Banting, Erinn.
  England. The land / Erinn Banting.
    p. cm. -- (Lands, peoples, and cultures series)
  Includes index.
  ISBN 0-7787-9321-4 (RLB) -- ISBN 0-7787-9689-2 (pbk)
    1. England--Description and travel--Juvenile literature.
2. Landscape--England--Juvenile literature. 3. Land use--England--Juvenile literature. I. Title. II. Series.
  DA632.B36 2004
  914.2--dc22
                                2004000814
                                LC

Contents

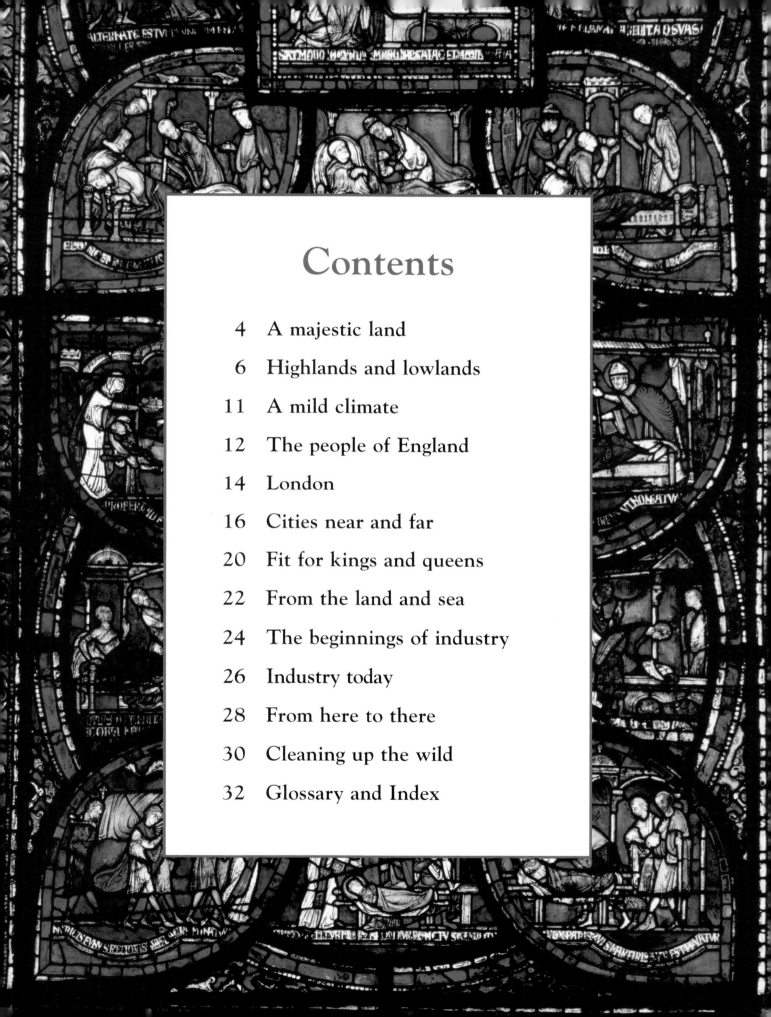

(above) People and traffic crowd the streets of Bowness-on-Windmere, a town in northern England.

From above, England looks like a patchwork quilt made of many squares. Each square is a farmer's field, where crops such as wheat and beets grow. Between the farms are lush valleys, rolling green hills, **bogs**, **moors**, and mountains. Along with Scotland to the north and Wales to the southwest, this green land occupies the island of Great Britain. Great Britain is part of a country called the United Kingdom, which includes Northern Ireland. Northern Ireland shares an island with the Republic of Ireland, to the west.

The center of it all

England takes up 54 percent of Great Britain, but it has an area of only 50,363 square miles (130,440 square kilometers). A person can drive from Nottingham, in central England, to any corner of England in a day. Despite its small size, England has been a leader in industry, trade, and exploration. From fierce conquerors who wanted to control the powerful land, to **immigrants** looking for a better life, people have wanted to live in England for centuries.

Facts at a glance
Official name: England
Area: 50,363 square miles (130,440 square kilometers)
Population: 49,138,839
Capital: London
Official language: English
Main religion: Church of England (Anglicanism)
Currency: British pound sterling
National holiday: St. George's Day (April 23)

More than half of England borders water, and England is home to some of the largest ports in the world. In villages such as Dorset, in the south, a majority of people make their living as fishers.

England is one of the most industrialized places in the world. At this power plant, electricity is made to power factories and homes.

Cattle munch grass on a rolling plain in southwestern England.

Highlands and lowlands

Low mountains cross the English landscape from the northwest to the southeast, where they become hills and flat plateaus. Across these highlands and lowlands stretch green valleys called dales, marshlands filled with plants and animals, mossy moors, and plains with forests or farms.

How England was formed

Tens of thousands of years ago, a land bridge, or giant strip of land, connected Great Britain to the rest of Europe. England's mountains were part of a range that ran from Norway, a country to the north, to Northern Ireland. Around 10,000 years ago, when the last **Ice Age** ended, large, slow-moving chunks of ice, called glaciers, began to melt and move across Europe. They eroded, or wore away, parts of England's highlands and formed the lower hills and plateaus in the south.

As the glaciers melted, the waters around Great Britain rose and covered the land bridge. Today, the North Sea separates Great Britain from Norway, Denmark, Germany, the Netherlands, and Belgium; the English Channel separates Great Britain from France; and the Celtic and Irish Seas separate Great Britain from Ireland.

England's highest point is Scafell Pike, which rises to 3,210 feet (978 meters). Scafell Pike is part of the Cumbrian Mountains, a branch of the Pennines in the northwest.

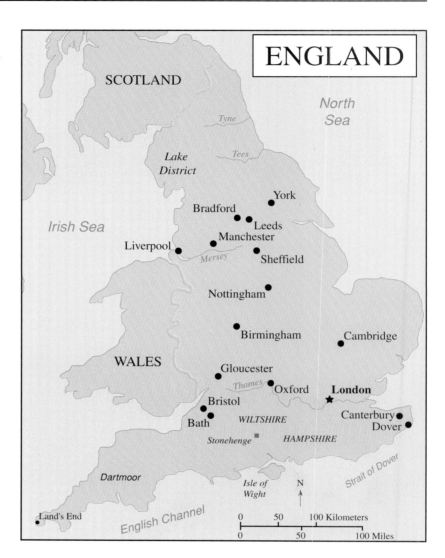

Mountains and valleys

The mountains that remain in England are part of a range called the Pennine Mountains, which begin in Scotland and run south to Derbyshire, a region in central England. The Pennine Mountains are called "the backbone of England" because the bumpy, unbroken range divides the island like a spine. The rugged mountains are rocky with little **fertile** soil. Most peaks are covered by thick grass and coarse, spiny bushes called gorse.

Northern lakes

The Cumbrian Mountains, in the northwest, shelter an area called the Lake District. The sixteen major lakes in the district formed at the end of the last Ice Age, when glaciers melted and valleys that they had carved out filled with water. Lake Windermere is the largest lake in the district. It is more than ten miles (sixteen kilometers) long and one mile (1.6 kilometers) wide.

Rivers

Many English rivers begin their journeys in the mountains, lakes, or lowland areas where water gathers. The rivers flow toward the coasts and into the sea. Many cities were built along the rivers, which were used to transport people and **cargo**. For centuries, the River Thames, which is the main river in southern England, has provided the people of London and surrounding areas with food, water, a means of transportation, and a place for leisure activities, such as boating. It winds for 205 miles (330 kilometers) near the ruins of forts and castles, through farmland, and through cities filled with factories, office buildings, and homes.

People visit Lake Windermere and the national park surrounding it to hike, boat, swim, and climb Scafell Pike and the surrounding mountains.

Downs and moors

Southern and eastern England have areas of grassy, treeless plains broken by low hills, which are called downs. In southcentral England, the largest downs are the Berkshire, Hampshire, and Marlborough Downs. In the southeast are the North Downs.

Moors stretch southwest of the downs. A moor is a wide area that is often covered in heath, which are low shrubs with small flowers, and with peat bogs. Peat bogs are swampy areas that were once low, shallow lakes. Over time, the plants and mud decomposed, or broke down, and formed a spongy material called peat. The peat built up in layers until the lakes were completely filled in.

(above) "The White Cliffs of Dover" is a popular English folksong written about the limestone landmark in southeastern England.

The White Cliffs of Dover

The Strait of Dover is the narrowest section of the English Channel, in the southeast. Rising 820 feet (250 meters) above the Strait of Dover are the White Cliffs of Dover. Over hundreds of millions of years, small hard-shelled animals called plankton attached themselves to the shoreline, died, and left their skeletons behind. Other plankton attached themselves to the skeletons and formed new layers, which eventually hardened into white cliffs made of a soft rock called limestone. Scientists estimate that the cliffs have grown by 49 feet (15 meters) over 100 million years.

Peat bogs and heath are not the only types of landscape found in England's moors. The three main moors — Dartmoor, Exmoor, and Bodmin — are also home to forests, grasslands, farms, and villages.

Flowers grow as far as the eye can see in part of the Fens in southeastern England.

The Fens

Marshes and **scrubland** once covered an area in southeastern England now called the Fens. For thousands of years, seawater flooded this low, flat land. **Minerals** from the seawater made the soil fertile, but there was too much water to grow crops. In the mid 1600s, sewers and windmills were built to drain and pump water from the area. After this, farmers were able to grow vegetables and other crops on the land. Today, mechanical pumps drain the Fens, but the threat of flooding still exists. Some scientists believe that if the ice in the **North Pole** continues to melt, the sea will rise within the next hundred years and permanently flood the Fens.

Land's End

Sandy beaches and windswept stone cliffs form the southwestern tip of England, called Land's End. Gray seals bask in the sun along the shores as dolphins splash and leap through the waves. Land's End is also a site of mystery and myth. According to legend, the warrior King Arthur is said to have fought his final battle at Land's End.

Many people visit Land's End as part of a challenge to travel from one end of Great Britain to the other. Land's End is the southernmost point of their journey, and John O'Groats, in Scotland, is the northernmost point. People have made this trip on foot, in wheelbarrows, on bicycles, on motorcycles, and in cars. The record for walking is twelve days, and the record for cycling is 44 hours. One man even tried to crawl while he pushed a pea with his nose. It hurt his nose so much that he gave up after only one mile (1.6 kilometers)!

Living fences

Low fences, some of which are thousands of years old, divide much of England's countryside. These fences, called hedgerows, were first built by the Anglo-Saxons, a group of warriors from Germany and Scandinavia who arrived in England around 410 A.D. As they gained control of sections of land, they protected their property with walls made from wooden stakes and spiny plants. Dead hedgerows, as these fences were called, were eventually replaced by fences made from live bushes and trees.

Recently, people building large farms and homes in the countryside have destroyed many live hedgerows. Other people are working to save the hedgerows, which are home to a variety of wildlife, including birds, butterflies, hedgehogs, and hares.

Off the coasts

The Isles of Scilly are a group of a hundred islands and rocks off Land's End. Only five of the Isles of Scilly are inhabited because of the threat of tall waves and winds that blow in from the ocean. St. Mary's, the only island where people live year-round, is home to the main port from which goods and people are transported to and from the other islands. It is farther south than the rest of England, so it has a warmer climate. When snow falls in parts of England, tropical trees and flowers are in full bloom on St. Mary's. The Isle of Wight, off the southwestern coast, is the largest island along England's shores.

The Channel Islands

Guernsey, Jersey, Alderney, and Sark are a group of islands in the English Channel known as the Channel Islands. They are owned by the United Kingdom, but each island governs itself. Guernsey, the second largest of the islands, even has its own **currency**, which it uses in addition to the British pound sterling. The islands, which were once owned by France, have a **culture** that blends English and French customs. Many people speak both French and English, celebrate French holidays, and enjoy French foods such as *moules à la marinière*, or mussels cooked in wine sauce.

Islands around the world

The United Kingdom claims ownership of territory in other parts of the world. These areas, which are mainly islands, are called British Overseas Territory. The territory includes islands in the Caribbean Sea, including Bermuda and the Cayman Islands; in the Indian Ocean, including the Chagos Archipelago; in the Irish Sea, including the Isle of Man; and in the Pacific Ocean, including the Pitcairn Islands. Some countries feel that they, rather than the United Kingdom, should have control over parts of the British Overseas Territory. For example, both Spain and the United Kingdom claim ownership of Gibraltar, an area on the southern tip of Spain.

Homes, offices, and buildings crowd the coast of Saint Peter's Port on the island of Guernsey, one of the Channel Islands.

A mild climate

Temperatures in England are fairly mild, averaging 36° Fahrenheit (2° Celsius) in the winter and 68° Fahrenheit (20° Celsius) in the summer. Snow falls in many parts of England during the winter, but it usually melts quickly. England owes its mild climate to the Gulf Stream, a warm air and water current that travels from the Caribbean Sea, in the south, across the Atlantic Ocean to England.

Rain and sun

"Red sky at night, shepherds delight. Red sky at morning, shepherds take warning" is an old saying that many English still use to predict the weather. It means that if the sky is red at sunset, the next day will be clear. If the sky is red at daybreak, it will probably rain that day. It is actually quite difficult to predict the weather in England. The sky can change from sunny to stormy in minutes because of strong winds that blow clouds and rain in from the Atlantic Ocean. Rain showers may last only minutes at a time, but they happen nearly every day.

More rain falls on the western coast than on the eastern coast because of the moist winds that blow in from the Atlantic. The average rainfall in the west is 58 inches (147 centimeters) a year, and the average in the east is 33 inches (84 centimeters) a year.

Flooding

Some English cities and towns stand on flood or coastal plains. These areas along the banks of rivers or coasts sometimes flood during heavy rainstorms, when rivers, streams, and seas cannot hold the extra water. The water rushes onto the plains, destroying homes, businesses, and farmland. Flooding happens mainly on the southwestern and southeastern coasts between September and April.

Brighton Beach, overlooking the English Channel in southern England, is a popular spot for people to sit and enjoy the warm weather.

The Thames estuary, which is the mouth of the River Thames, sometimes floods between September and April.

11

The people of England

Farmers at a market in the Lake District, in the northwest, display sheep and other animals for sale.

Most people in England are **descended** from the Anglo-Saxons, who came from Denmark and northwestern Germany beginning in the 400s. They spoke a version of English that developed into the language spoken today.

Living in different regions

England is divided into geographic regions. Over the course of history, different peoples settled in each region, influencing the customs, traditions, and languages there. For example, in Cornwall, an area in the southwestern region of West Country, people speak Cornish. Cornish is a dialect of Gaelic, the language spoken by the Celts, who settled in the region around 700 B.C. People in the eastern region of East Anglia have been influenced by German culture because the area was settled by the Angles, a Germanic people.

Each region of England also has its own foods, many of which use ingredients produced locally. The people of Yorkshire, in the east, make a type of pastry called Yorkshire pudding from flour, animal fat, eggs, and milk. The pudding, which is served covered in gravy, was first made as a way to fill people up when meat was scarce. In East Anglia, farmers invented a dish called jugged hare in an effort to get rid of hares eating their crops. The hares are cooked in a tall jug set in a deep pan of boiling water.

The tradition of wearing school uniforms began in England hundreds of years ago. Most English children still wear uniforms to school, including a blazer and tie.

Grandparents play ball with their grandchildren outside their home in southwestern England. Some English families live in modern houses, while others live in homes that are hundreds of years old.

Many people have moved to England from islands in the Caribbean. A Caribbean festival full of music and dance called the Notting Hill Festival takes place at the end of August in the London neighborhood of Notting Hill.

Other arrivals

People from other countries brought new cultures and traditions to England. During the 1400s, French and Jewish people came to England from other parts of Europe to escape religious **persecution**. Irish settlers also moved to England because of religious persecution and to avoid a **famine** that ravaged their country in the 1800s. People in England's major cities celebrate Irish holidays, such as St. Patrick's Day, which honors one of Ireland's **patron saints**.

During the early 1900s, immigrants from countries such as Poland, Hungary, and Romania flooded England's borders when their own countries were torn apart by war. In the late 1940s, when British **colonies**, such as India, parts of Africa, and islands in the Caribbean Sea, won their independence from the United Kingdom, immigrants from these places came to England in search of work. Both London and Birmingham have large Indian and Jamaican populations, while London also has large groups of people from Bangladesh, South Africa, Nigeria, and Zimbabwe.

London

(above) The Tower of London has served as a fortress, prison, and home to kings and queens. Today, the crown jewels, a collection of precious gems and objects owned by the monarchy, are carefully guarded there.

Since the time of the Celts, the city of London has been an important historical, political, cultural, and financial center. *Llyndun*, a Celtic word that means "high-lying fort," was the name of an early **fortification** built where modern-day London stands. When armies from the **Roman Empire** arrived in England in the first century A.D., they conquered the Celtic settlement and renamed it Londinium. Today, England's capital city has grown into a region that is divided into 33 sections, two of which are the City of London and the City of Westminster.

Places of power

For hundreds of years, kings, queens, and elected politicians have ruled England from London. The Houses of Parliament are a group of buildings where England's government meets to make important decisions. Big Ben is the nickname given to the enormous bell that hangs in the clock tower at the Houses of Parliament.

Big Ben rings on the hour, quarter-hour, and half-hour each day. The bell has been broadcast on the radio since 1923, so people throughout England can set their clocks and watches to Big Ben's time.

Buckingham Palace has been the residence of England's monarchy since 1837. Today, parts of the castle are open so visitors can see how England's kings and queens live.

Palaces

Buckingham Palace is the London home of England's **monarchy** and the building in which the royal family's offices are located. The monarchy no longer holds true power but the Queen is the country's head of state, or symbolic ruler, and she participates in important ceremonies and celebrations. Many of these ceremonies take place in Buckingham Palace's throne room, a beautifully decorated red and gold room that houses the monarchs' thrones.

Nearby Kensington Palace was home to England's rulers until 1760. The palace still has rooms where members of the royal family live and work.

A religious center

Churches are among the oldest buildings in London. Rising high above the rooftops is the great dome of St. Paul's Cathedral. The cathedral was engulfed in flames during the Great Fire of London, which destroyed much of the city in 1666, but it was rebuilt between 1675 and 1710. St. Paul's dome, which is one of the largest domes in the world, is topped by a tower that contains the Golden Gallery, from which nearly all of London can be seen.

The oldest church in England is Westminster Abbey, where England's monarchs, important politicians, religious leaders, and poets are buried or honored with tombs and monuments. The coronations, or crownings, of new kings or queens also take place at Westminster Abbey.

Cities throughout England grew from the settlements of ancient peoples, such as the Celts and Romans. Today, each city is a mixture of new and old, where modern factories and offices stand next to stone churches, homes, and walls built hundreds and even thousands of years ago. More than 75 percent of the population lives in the busy cities of England's interior and along the coasts.

Birmingham

The people of Birmingham call their western city "Brum," and they are called "Brummies." Birmingham is known as an industrial city. Factories that once produced parts for ships now manufacture cars and car parts. The Cadbury plant makes world-famous chocolate, and Wedgewood China manufactures blue and white porcelain dishes, vases, and figurines.

(above) Two statues of liver birds with their wings spread wide perch atop Liverpool's best-known building, the Liver Building (background). Legend says that if the birds fly away, the city will disappear.

Liverpool

The city of Liverpool stands at the mouth of the Mersey River, on the western coast. The people who live in Liverpool, or Liverpudlians, say that the city's name comes from mythical birds, called liver birds, that once flew along the Mersey River. The liver bird is now the city's symbol.

Liverpool became extremely wealthy during the 1800s as ships from Ireland, North America, and the Caribbean arrived daily in its harbor carrying goods such as cotton, sugar, and timber. Liverpool later experienced many difficult years as shipping declined, but England's government is working to restore the city to its former productivity. The Albert Dock, which is part of the harbor, has been rebuilt and the warehouses once used to store cargo have been restored and turned into apartments, restaurants, and shops.

Politicians meet at the Birmingham Council House, which was built between 1874 and 1879, to discuss how to run the city.

York

York, in the northeast, was a headquarters for the Roman army beginning in the first century A.D. Ancient stone streets from the Roman city are now buried, but there are still traces of walls that once protected the army from attack. In 886 A.D., the Vikings, who sailed from the north, invaded the settlement and named it Jorvik, pronounced "Yorvik," which was eventually shortened to York. The modern Jorvik Viking Center was built on the original Viking settlement. Visitors to the center can walk down a reconstruction of Viking streets, see craftspeople make jewelry and clothing as Vikings did, and examine the hundreds of **artifacts** found at the site.

Beneath the streets of central York is another reminder of the city's history, the York Dungeons. The dungeons were used as a prison during the **Middle Ages**, when many people were tortured and killed because of their religious beliefs.

(above) Streetcars transport passengers through downtown Manchester. The city is home to the oldest passenger railway station still standing in the world, built in 1830.

Manchester

Weavers from Belgium, a country east of England, settled in the northwestern city of Manchester in the 1300s. There, they produced wool and linen fabric, clothing, and blankets. By the 1800s, **textiles** made in Manchester were being sold throughout the world. People from Manchester no longer produce as many textiles, but they manufacture parts for airplanes, ships, computers, and other electronic equipment.

The York Minster Cathedral, in York, was built in the Gothic style, with arches pointing toward heaven, ribbed vaulting to support the ceiling, and the largest stained glass window in the world.

Bath

Bath, in the south, was founded by the Romans, who discovered underground hot springs filled with minerals nearby. They built wells and pumps so they could control the springs' flow of water and use it in public bathhouses, which gave the city its name. People soaking in the baths believed that the minerals in the water cured their ailments. Although some modern spas use the hot springs, only one of the original Roman baths, the Great Bath, still stands and is now a museum.

(below) Bath's Pump Room, built by the Romans to control the flow of water into the baths, is now a restaurant.

(above) The Nottingham Council House, which is where offices of the city's government are housed, has a bell in it that is nicknamed "Little John" after one of Robin Hood's Merry Men.

Nottingham

Nottingham, a city in central England, is best known for a nearby forest that was home to one of England's most famous heroes, Robin Hood. No one is sure if Robin Hood really existed, but according to legend, he and his companions, called his Merry Men, lived in Sherwood Forest, which was a royal hunting ground. There, they stole from the rich to give to the poor.

In the 1300s and 1400s, shortly after Robin Hood supposedly lived, people built nearly 400 caves and passageways beneath Nottingham. Most were used as homes, storerooms, wells, and breweries, where beer was made and kept cool. During World War II, other caves were built as shelters where people could hide if the city was under attack. Today, visitors to Nottingham can tour the abandoned caves.

Canterbury

Gates, churches, and other buildings from the Middle Ages still stand in Canterbury, in the southeast. Millions of **pilgrims** flock to the city each year to visit the Canterbury Cathedral, where Thomas Becket, a leader of the Roman Catholic Church, was murdered in 1164. In streets around the cathedral stand half-timbered buildings, made in the Middle Ages by filling wooden frames with clay mixed with straw or dung. These buildings, which were once homes, have been restored and are now restaurants and shops.

(right) The southcentral city of Oxford is home to Oxford University, the oldest English-speaking university in the world. The Bodleian Library, at Oxford, adds more than 300,000 books and other documents to its collection each year.

People crowd Kent Street in downtown Canterbury on their way to shops and restaurants.

Throughout England stand castles built by **noble** families and invaders to protect the land they conquered. Many of England's castles are in ruins, but some still stand and are the homes of wealthy families. Other castles are now hotels and museums.

Windsor Castle

Windsor Castle was built more than 900 years ago by King William the Conqueror. Over the centuries, other kings and queens rebuilt and expanded the castle. In the 1170s, the Round Tower was constructed at the center of the castle. Attackers who got past the castle's thick walls and iron gates could not reach the tower, which was surrounded by a moat, or deep ditch.

The royal family still lives in Windsor Castle for parts of the year, but many sections of the castle are open to the public. People can visit St. George's Chapel, where ten past kings and queens are buried, and the Semi-State Rooms, which contain **tapestries**, sculptures, and paintings by some of the world's most famous artists.

Some visitors to Warwick Castle claim that the ghost of Sir Fulke Grenville, a noble who lived in the castle and was stabbed by an angry servant in 1628, haunts the rooms where he once slept, now called The Ghost Tower.

Warwick Castle

Warwick Castle, in central England, was originally a hilltop settlement built in 914 by the Anglo-Saxons. A rampart, or wall with towers spaced along it for defense, surrounded the settlement. Stone buildings replaced Warwick's original wooden structures in the 1100s, and for hundreds of years many kings, queens, and nobles lived there. In 1978, the castle was turned into a museum.

In 1992, a fire broke out in part of Windsor Castle that destroyed more than a hundred rooms. The castle was opened to visitors to raise the money for the renovations, which were completed in 1997.

Leeds Castle

Leeds Castle, outside London, was built in the 1100s across two islands on a lake. It later became known as "the Lady's Castle" because six queens lived there. A thick wall surrounded the castle and people could only enter through a gatehouse. Soldiers in the gatehouse tower shot arrows or dropped stones and boiling oil on invaders below. The gatehouse also had a drawbridge, which could be raised or lowered to allow people to cross the water to the castle. Today, the castle is privately owned, but visitors can see some of the rooms and explore a maze made from hedgerows.

Castle Howard

Construction of Castle Howard, northeast of York, began in 1699 and ended more than a hundred years later. The castle is named after the Howards, a noble family whose descendants still live there today. Hundreds of rooms, including living quarters, kitchens, music rooms, art galleries, and a ballroom, fill the main house. The castle grounds have forests, gardens, lakes, and monuments, including a pyramid and a temple.

The lake surrounding Leeds Castle provided a natural defense from attackers.

The exterior of Castle Howard is decorated with statues of characters from Greek mythology.

 # From the land and sea

English farms grow crops such as wheat, barley, potatoes, beets, and rape, a grain used to make canola oil. There are also green pastures where livestock, such as cows and sheep, graze. For a long time, agriculture and fishing were England's main industries, but today only two percent of English people work in the fields and in the seas.

(top) Once wheat fields are cut, machines called combines separate the grains from the stalks.

(below) A worker sorts apples at a factory in Kent, in southeastern England.

Wheat

Throughout England's countryside, golden stalks of wheat blow in the gentle breezes. Farmers plow their fields and plant the wheat seeds in April. Then in August, they cut, bundle, and ship the wheat to local mills to be turned into flour. Wheat and flour have long been important to England's economy. Many castles even had their own flour mills, which were made from enormous stone slabs turned by water-powered wheels. Today, mills use modern machinery to grind wheat into flour.

Livestock

Sheep graze throughout England, particularly in the rugged hills of the north and west and in the greener pastures of the south. After the sheep's wool is shorn, or cut, it is combed, dyed, and spun into cloth. England is famous for its wool and wool products. The rough wool from short-haired sheep is made into hats, suits, and blankets. The wool from long-haired sheep is used to make softer items, including sweaters.

Cows grazing in fields separated by hedgerows or low fences are also common throughout the English countryside. The brown Jersey and Guernsey cows, named after the Channel Islands where they were first bred, produce a creamy milk that is also made into butter and cheese. Black-and-white or brown Herefords and the spotted Shorthorns are famous for their tender beef.

Jersey cows graze on grass and weeds at a dairy farm in southwestern England.

Mad cows?

A disease commonly called "mad cow disease" emerged in the United Kingdom in 1986. Scientists believe the disease is caused when cattle, who are grass and grain eaters, eat feed made from the parts of other animals. Cattle infected by the disease became ill and died. People who ate infected meat also became sick. Many countries stopped buying cattle or meat from the United Kingdom, and cattle farmers lost a lot of money. In 2001, the United Kingdom was hit by another disease, called "hoof and mouth disease," which swept through cattle, pig, and sheep farms. Farmers were forced to kill millions of animals to prevent the spread of the disease. Today, many countries have strict rules about accepting cattle from the United Kingdom, and farmers in the United Kingdom are very careful to monitor and test their animals to control these diseases.

Fishing

The waters around England are filled with many types of fish. Fishers off the southern coast return with bushels of different types of fish, such as sole and plaice. Along the eastern and western shores, fish such as mackerel, herring, and cod are the main catches. Most fish caught in England is sold in local markets and grocery stores, and some is **exported** to France.

Fishers unload a catch of mackerel onto their ship off the coast of Cornwall, in southwestern England.

The beginnings of industry

Between 1760 and 1830, the Industrial Revolution changed the way goods were produced and farmers worked their fields. The Industrial Revolution began in England, where new inventions and sources of energy made jobs such as harvesting and spinning wool easier and quicker. Thousands of factories sprung up in cities such as Manchester, Birmingham, and Liverpool to produce machine-made items that people once created by hand. Machines also replaced many workers on farms, so people from the countryside flocked to cities to work in factories.

The steam engine

The invention that started it all was the steam engine, which used steam to create power. James Watt, a Scottish inventor who worked in England, based his design on a smaller engine created in 1712 by English inventor Thomas Newcomen. Watt's engine, invented in 1765, was faster, more efficient, and able to power machines that shaped metal, cut wood, or spun fabric. A unit of energy called a "watt" is named after James Watt.

Coal

Coal mining become a major industry in the 1700s, when coal was discovered in the Pennine Mountains. As more machines powered by steam engines were built during the Industrial Revolution, demand for coal, which was burned to heat the water in steam engines, increased. Miners began to search for and discover coal in other parts of England. By the 1800s, there were 170 coal mines in England. Cities in mining areas grew as more factories opened.

Coal mines

Coal mines were very unsafe. Many mines collapsed, trapping and killing thousands of miners. Other miners, as well as people who lived in cities where factories burned coal, developed breathing problems and lung disease.

"Killer fogs," or thick, green fogs caused by coal smoke, also killed plants and animals. Today, only two coal mines remain open in England. Cleaner and safer sources of fuel, such as hydroelectric power, which creates electricity from running water, are used instead.

How a steam engine works

Pump

◇ Valve
— Hot steam
═ Cooled steam/water
▬ Water from well

1. Burning coal heats up water to create steam.
2. The steam fills a chamber and pushes up a piece of metal called a piston.
3. A valve holds the steam in the chamber.
4. The valve opens, and the steam rushes into a separate chamber. As the steam escapes, the piston drops down.
5. The rising and falling of the piston creates power, which is sent to other parts of the machine.

A miner uses a shovel to dig for coal in a northeastern mine, in this photograph from the mid-1900s.

Textiles

Making textiles was a major industry in England by the 1700s, but new inventions during the Industrial Revolution changed the way spinners, knitters, and weavers worked. The flying shuttle, invented in 1733 by a man from England named John Kay, improved looms so that weavers could weave more quickly and easily. The shuttles, or pieces of wood, were attached to two strings that weavers held in front of them. When the weavers pulled the strings, the shuttles "flew," or moved quickly back and forth, and wove yarn into cloth. This invention replaced shuttles that weavers passed through the loom by hand.

As weaving machines became faster and easier, new types of cloth developed. In 1844, English inventor John Mercer found a way to make cotton cloth that was easier to clean and more durable than wool. This new type of cloth, called mercerized cotton after its inventor, was created by coating cotton fibers with chemicals that made the cotton smoother and shinier. Demand for this cloth grew, and in the 1800s and 1900s England became the world's largest producer and exporter of both woolen and cotton textiles.

Factory workers weave fabric on machines in 1844.

Industry today

England's industries have changed many times since the 1700s. Today, England manufactures fewer textiles and machines and more electronics, automobiles, and pharmaceuticals, or medicines. More than 50 percent of the population works in service industries, such as tourism, education, and sales.

Made in factories

Products made in England's factories are sold throughout the world. England is known for its fine cars, such as Jaguar and Rolls-Royce, which were first manufactured in the 1920s and 1930s. Today, Jaguar still operates in the United Kingdom, but is owned by the Ford Motor Company, an American company. Rolls-Royce Motor Cars is now owned by the German company BMW. Rolls-Royce is still based in England and manufactures engines for airplanes, and jets. England also has many companies that manufacture computer parts and micro-electronics, including parts for robots.

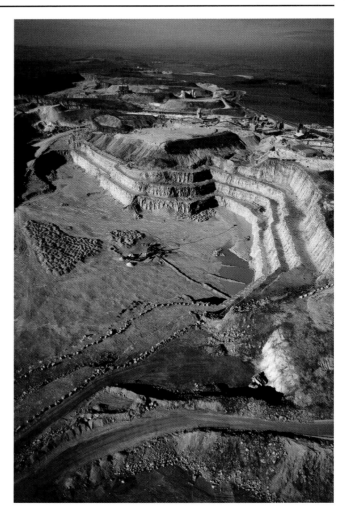

Sand, gravel, limestone, and crushed rock are mined in England for the construction industry.

Making medicine

When Alexander Fleming, a Scottish doctor and professor who lived in England, left for a two-week vacation in 1928, he forgot to put away one of his experiments. When he returned, he found mold growing on his experiment and noticed that the mold had kept away bacteria, or germs. He used the mold to make a drug called penicillin, which has cured millions of people around the world of infections and diseases. Research and the manufacturing of medicines have been central to England's economy since Alexander Fleming's time.

A welder builds part of a subway car at a factory in York.

Visiting England

One of England's largest industries is tourism. Millions of people visit England each year to see its historic cathedrals and castles and to explore the beautiful landscape. One of the most popular tourist spots is Stonehenge, a mysterious circle of giant stone slabs that is thousands of years old. No one is sure how ancient peoples moved the enormous rocks to the area or arranged them in the circle.

A worker inspects capsules before they are bottled at a pharmaceutical company.

Beautiful and strong

Porcelain is one of the finest types of clay for making dishes, figurines, and other decorative items. In the 1800s, Josiah Spode II, who was from England, created a thin, very durable type of porcelain called bone china. Bone china was made by mixing a white type of clay, called china clay, with bone ash, a fine powder created when cattle bones are burned. The English company Royal Doulton uses bone china to make its famous painted plates and figurines. Josiah Wedgwood, who founded the company called Wedgwood, made another type of pottery called Jasper Ware. Jasper Ware is usually blue with white raised decorations. People still buy valuable porcelain or pottery from Royal Doulton and Wedgewood, often as part of a large collection.

Some of the dishware made by Wedgwood is carefully painted by hand.

During the Industrial Revolution, **canals** and rail lines were built to move English-made goods throughout England and to ports along the coasts. From there, the goods were shipped around the world. New types of trains and ships were constructed that carried heavier loads and traveled more quickly. George Stephenson invented the steam **locomotive** in 1814, and the Great Western steamship was launched in 1837. Both were powered by steam engines.

Some double-decker buses are open on top so visitors can easily see the city.

On the road

North American drivers might find driving in England a little confusing because, unlike North Americans, who drive on the right side of the road, the English drive on the left. In England, taxis often have foldable seats behind the front seats that flip down to make room for extra passengers. Bright red double-decker buses are another common sight. Tourists often ride on the top story so they can see more of the sights.

The Tower Bridge was built between 1886 and 1894 to link southeastern and eastern London. The bridge is raised and lowered so that tall ships can pass.

Traveling the tube

When people in England say they are going on "the Underground" or "the Tube," they mean the subway. The first underground railway in the world was built in London in 1863 and ran for about four miles (six kilometers). Today, trains zip over 254 miles (408 kilometers) of tracks above and below ground.

The Chunnel

For a very long time, boats were the only way for people to travel across the English Channel to France. To make the trip faster and easier, "the Channel Tunnel," or "Chunnel," was completed in 1994. High-speed trains run through a 31-mile (50-kilometer) underwater tunnel, carrying people, cargo, cars, and buses. The Chunnel now connects Folkstone, England and Calais, France.

Chunnel trains reach speeds of up to 100 miles (160 kilometers) per hour.

Many people have crossed the English Channel by hovercraft, a boat that sits on a large inflatable tube. An English engineer named Christopher Cockerell invented the hovercraft, which can also travel on land, in 1956.

29

Fossils found in England prove that crocodiles, elephants, and rhinoceroses lived there millions of years ago. Wolves, bears, and wild boars later inhabited the island's dense forests. These animals and many others no longer live in England because of climate change, hunting, and because their homes in the forests were destroyed when trees were cut down for **timber**. Coal smoke and the use of **pesticides** on crops have also damaged natural **habitats**.

The government is now working to save England's plants and animals. Farmers receive money if they turn parts of their farmland into forested conservation areas, and hunters are only allowed to hunt certain animals during specific seasons. Laws restricting the use of coal and pesticides help control pollution and keep the green fields and animals of England's countryside healthy.

Many people make furniture and crafts from antlers that red deer have shed.

Mammals

England's hedgerows rustle with the movements of hedgehogs, rabbits, and field mice. Below many hedgerows, rabbits dig deep burrows that sometimes have hundreds of tunnels and chambers. There, they hide from foxes and other **predators**.

Deer are the most common wild mammals in England. There are two main types — the red deer and the Chinese water deer. Red deer get their name from the reddish-brown color of their hides. The males have huge antlers, which they shed each spring. Chinese water deer are smaller and are the only species of deer that does not grow antlers. They were brought to the London Zoo from China in the 1800s and now live in the wild.

Seals bask in the sun along cliffs on the western coast. Seals were once used for their fat and skin, but they are now protected by the English government and hunting is illegal.

Birdwatching

Some birds, such as kestrels, swallows, and robins, live in the countryside, hunting for worms to feed their young. Other birds, such as gulls, puffins, and ducks, live on the sides of rocky cliffs or in caves along the coasts. The mute swan, which is white with black markings around its eyes and an orange beak, is the largest bird in England. These swans are called mute, or silent, because they rarely make any noise. At one time, most swans were the property of the king or queen. For this reason, swans are known as "royal birds."

Glorious gardens

England's countryside is filled with wildflowers, such as primroses, bluebells, daffodils, buttercups, and campions. England's earliest gardens were filled with these flowers, which were allowed to grow wild. In the 1600s and 1700s, more formal gardens became popular. They had stone paths, fountains, and neat rows of plants, trees, and bushes, some cut to look like statues.

Giant lily pads float in an indoor pond at The Royal Botanic Garden at Kew, near London.

Tropical plants

Today, some English gardeners grow plants and trees that are particular to their region. On Tresco, one of the Isles of Scilly, plants such as lobster claws and trees such as flame trees grow in a garden that was once part of a **monastery**. Nowhere else in England has the warm climate that these plants and trees require.

Puffins, which have red and yellow bills, live on islands off England's eastern coast.

Glossary

artifact A product, usually historical, made by human craft

bog Soft, water-soaked areas of land

canal A man-made river

cargo Goods transported by ship, plane, train, or truck

colony An area controlled by a distant country

culture The customs, beliefs, and arts of a distinct group of people

currency Money

descended Having roots to a certain family or group

export To sell goods to another country

famine An extreme shortage of food

fertile Able to produce abundant crops or vegetation

fortification A strong building constructed to resist attacks

habitat The area or environment in which plants or animals are normally found

Ice Age A period of thousands or millions of years when thick ice covers large areas of land

immigrant A person who settles in another country

locomotive A self-propelled vehicle that pushes or pulls railroad cars

Middle Ages The period in western European history from about 500 A.D. to 1500 A.D.

mineral A naturally occurring, non-living substance obtained through mining

monarchy A government that is ruled by a king, queen, emperor, or empress

monastery A building where religious men called monks live and work

moor An area of countryside covered with rough grass and moss

noble A person born into a high social class

North Pole The most northern point at which Earth tilts on its axis

patron saint A saint who is believed to protect a person, profession, city, or country

persecution The act of harming another person for religious, racial, or political reasons

pesticide A chemical that kills weeds and insects

pilgrim A person who makes a religious journey to a sacred place

predator An animal that kills and eats other animals

Roman Empire A group of countries and territories ruled by ancient Rome

scrubland An area of land that is uncultivated and covered with sparse stunted vegetation

tapestry A heavy, decorative weaving that hangs on walls

textile A fabric or cloth

timber Wood used to construct buildings, furniture, and other objects

 # Index

     1 2 3 4 5 6 7 8 9 0   Printed in the U.S.A.   3 2 1 0 9 8 7 6 5 4